The Classroom

Michael James D'Amato

iUniverse, Inc.
New York Lincoln Shanghai

The Classroom

iUniverse books may be ordered through booksellers or by contacting:

iUniverse
2021 Pine Lake Road, Suite 100
Lincoln, NE 68512
www.iuniverse.com
1-800-Authors (1-800-288-4677)

The cover art and illustrations were all created by high school senior Josephine Tam.

ISBN: 0-595-33783-X

Printed in the United States of America

This book is dedicated to my parents, Judith and Frank.
Thank you for showing me how to live poetically.

ACKNOWLEDGEMENTS

I would like to thank my parents. They have made more sacrifices for me and my brother than we will ever realize.

I would also like to thank Matthew Garcia, Maria Pizzelli, and Roberta Specht for enlightening my career path early on.

A warm thanks to Lee Gaskins for introducing me to the talented Josephine Tam.

Lastly, I would like to express my love for all my colleagues, family, friends, and students.

INTRODUCTION

"Ninety-nine percent of what you need to know about teaching was not taught to you in college." This was the first bit of advice I received from my mentor when I began my teaching career. It sounded bizarre at first, but in less than a week I felt exactly what he meant. Although my college courses offered some amazing theories, rarely did they provide anything of substance I could actually use in the classroom. This realization was the catalyst for writing *The Classroom*.

This book is broken down into fourteen chapters covering the most pivotal aspects of teaching. As an added bonus, at the end of each chapter, I included a few activities and ideas aimed to amaze your students. The pace of this book was based on the advice I received from a student during my first week as a new teacher, "Forget the fancy words." In other words, I cut right to the chase and created quick and convenient glances at several concepts you could apply to your classroom tomorrow.

In closing, we recently embarked on a new millennium and the number one teaching method used throughout the country is still the lecture model. It is time for a change.

CONTENTS

Chapter One—In the Beginning

1. "Education is not filling a pail, but the lighting of a fire." William Butler Yeats

2. You're Getting Warmer

When approaching a new audience it is a good idea to warm up to them first before you embark on your mission. Before you share your thoughts with a group of students, families, or colleagues, they desire to know something personal about you. Share an anecdote, genuine story, or my favorite, "This one time, at band camp…" Establish a *connection* to your listeners early on and your message should not fall on deaf ears.

For insight into Michael D'Amato, allow me to quickly share my favorite memory as a teacher. It was the time I stole from the rich and gave to the poor. First off, to establish setting, I teach in an urban school district with a population of forty thousand. There is not one book store in the entire city. With a three minute phone call, I was able to arrange for scholarships allowing two of my students to attend a month-long summer leadership program in an affluent neighborhood twenty minutes away.

3. Hook, Line, and Sinker

The typical lesson for each class should involve three parts: Hook, line, and sinker. Your first task when presenting a lesson is to pull the students into the lesson. This could be done with a simple question, "How did pigeons help the U.S. become victorious in World War II?" (The "hook" part of your lesson is often referred to as the anticipatory set.) Once you have your students interested/curious, then you should start to attack your objectives. At the end of each lesson, you want to allow a couple minutes for closure. This is the time when you want to make sure all of your main ideas have sunk into their memory properly. During the closure period is when you will get feedback on how well you reached your objectives.

A helpful way to focus your objectives is to categorize them into three areas: Knowledge, skills, and values. If you are teaching something and it doesn't fall into one of these areas, it is not "educational."

4. Mirror, Mirror, on the Wall

Who is the meanest of them all? I am. In the beginning of the year, preferably during the "first fifteen days" of class, I like to use a mirror analogy with my students. "If I am being nice to you, it's a reflection of what I see. If I am being firm with you, that too is a reflection of what I am seeing." (Note: It is better to refer to yourself as a firm teacher as opposed to a mean teacher.)

5. No Childhood Left Behind

Many of our students' childhoods have been stolen. Children are forced to grow up faster today than ever. What can you do about it, you ask? First off, stop showing those movies to eat time (we have all been there) and instead try an activity with them.

Throughout this book I will be offering a plethora of activities, brain teasers, and puzzles that I have successfully used with my students. Whether it is a specialty day the class earned, a day before a long break, or state-testing week, try an activity with them to strengthen the class chemistry. You will feel so much better about yourself and so will your students. Plus, it will do wonders for your rapport with them.

Still not convinced? Okay, here are three solid reasons why you should do an activity once in a while with your students. As stated before, our students are growing up too fast. Let's offer them some silly memories they will look back on and cherish. Secondly, teachers are constantly asking students to perform, but rarely give them back anything. All solid relationships are based on give and take. (In order to get money from the ATM machine, you have to make occasional deposits, right?) Finally, activities let students become comfortable in front of their peers, it helps build upon the class atmosphere, and it strengthens their risk-taking potential.

Another point I would like to talk about is semantics. First off, never use the word "games," they are *activities*. Word spreads fast when you are playing games in your classroom. Secondly, describe your activity as one focusing on problem solving, team building, conflict resolution, or there's my favorite phrase, an activity on multicultural appreciation.

6. Eureka!

Have you ever tried to help someone who didn't want your assistance? I am guessing his response was something like, "I can do it myself." Part of human nature is that we like solving problems. Most of the people I know enjoy a good mental challenge from time to time. Teachers need to use this innate quality in people to maximize their students' learning potential.

To best illustrate this notion, let us take a look at a very popular WWII photograph, with a relatively unknown twist. The key here is that instead of showing the picture and directly telling the students its meaning, allow them to "wrestle" with the challenge, giving guiding clues when necessary.

At the entrance of the Auschwitz concentration camp was a sign, "Arbeit Macht Frei." (Rough translation: "Work Makes One Free") Show the students the photograph and ask if they notice anything odd about the picture. Once they notice the anomaly, have them generate ideas as to why the "B" on the sign is deliberately upside down. It takes my average class about three to four minutes to reach the conclusion that when several Jewish metal workers were forced to make the sign, they intentionally put the letter upside down so others coming into the camp would know right away that something was terribly wrong.

By using "guided discovery" instead of force feeding, the information becomes more significant, more interesting, and more memorable. In addition, student learning is accompanied by a sense of achievement.

---

7. Brain Teaser

Which rock group has four members, all deceased, one was an author, one was assassinated, one was a father, and the last was a bear? *(Answers to brain teasers and puzzles are found at the end of each chapter.)*

8. An Activity on Multicultural Appreciation (Focusing on Team Building)

<u>Marshmallows</u>

Group size: 10-20
Age Group: 10 and up
Materials: Several pieces of large construction paper
Time: 20 to 30 minutes
Location: Large classroom, hallway, or outdoors
Skills: Teamwork, Leadership, Multicultural Appreciation, &
               Cooperation

a. First you need to create a start and finish line. They should be about twenty-five feet apart.

b. Give instructions: The entire group needs to move safely across a lake of hot chocolate, using marshmallows, without losing a member. (Between the start and finish line is the hot chocolate.) The team will start with five marshmallows (construction paper). The only way a person can successfully cross the hot chocolate is if a part of her body is touching a marshmallow. If a person touches the hot chocolate and is not on a marshmallow, she is lost. If a body part is not on the marshmallow, for even a split second, the marshmallow is lost. (During the activity, you are the monster who takes the marshmallows away if left unattended. You will need to be quick.) When you are ready to begin, hand out the marshmallows to a few students.

c. Other rules: Students may not drag, throw, or rip the marshmallows.

d. If a member is lost in the chocolate, as the facilitator you have a choice. Either she is out or the entire group has to start over. I would rather them start over at this point with different people going first.

e. When the team loses too many marshmallows and completing the task becomes impossible, allow them to start over with different students beginning with the construction paper. (Have extra paper just in case too many sheets rip.)

f. This is an activity where the loudest kids might try to get their way. You may also notice that shy students want to participate but are afraid of being put down.

g. If you want to be creative, bring a blindfold and have one student use it as a handicap.

h. Bring a camera.

i. Process the activity with the students when they finish. (Processing the activity means you allow the students to reflect on what they felt were the key components of the activity.) Ask the students questions about the difficulties they faced and what thoughts were going on in their minds. Ask them to relate this activity to life or school.

9. Fascinating Fact

People who don't vote in Cuba's national elections have a red X painted on the front door of their homes. (People who don't vote in Australia are fined approximately one hundred dollars.)

10. An Important Thing I Learned About Life is...

When you point a finger at someone, three fingers point right back at you.

Answer to #3—Homing pigeons saved the lives of hundreds, maybe thousands of U.S. soldiers who landed in enemy territory by not allowing their location to be picked up on radar.

Answer to #7—Mount Rushmore

Chapter Two—Bag of Tricks

11. **"It is a miracle that curiosity survives formal education."** Albert Einstein

12. Abby's Story

The following tale is my all-time favorite. Take a few moments to read it and I guarantee you will rush to share it with someone close to you.

The first thing I want you to do is visualize a land. Near the center of the land I want you to picture a long river. In this land lives a girl. She is an independent woman who lives on her own. One of the things Abby likes to do is gather the leftover scraps and feed them to the hungry piranhas.

One starry night by the river, Abby hears an unrecognizable voice from across the river calling out to her. She looks up and sees a charming boy. She answers by making a comment about the weather. Before she realizes it, they are engaged in a conversation like no other she has ever had. As the conversation continues at a brilliant pace, she becomes overwhelmed by the complexity of the mood and feels quite moved by the boy's presence. As the sky darkens, they realize they need to part ways before it gets too dark and the wolves come out. So they part in a way that they are both reassured they will see each other again soon. That night Abby does not get a wink of sleep. Her pounding heart keeps her up all night.

The next day she finds herself by the river. She is looking around the river for some evidence that last night wasn't imagined. And like a mirror image, she notices the boy seems to be doing the same. Without hesitation, they take up a conversation like yesterday's, but deeper. This time rain shortens their meeting. The two bid farewell and part into the night. On her way home she stops at the nearby boatman.

"How much would it take for you to bring me to the other side?" inquires Abby.

The boatman fondles his skinny beard and says, "Tell ya' what I can do for you. Jus' give me the deed to your home and the keys to your car and I will do you the favor." Based on the awkward reaction from Abby, the boatman justifies his price by reminding the girl of his very busy schedule and the bad economy. Abby says she will think about it. On her way home she decides to stop at her aunt's house on the hill.

As she approaches her aunt's house, she notices her aunt is sitting on the porch in a rocking chair, half asleep. As the girl approaches, the aunt becomes aware of her presence and perks up. The aunt quickly notices Abby is walking heavier than usual. Abby greets her aunt and the aunt immediately notices her pleasant demeanor. "So tell me about this boy," the aunt suggests. The girl goes on to discuss her dilemma and brightens at each turn. Abby goes on to tell her that she consulted the boatman and the aunt quickly comments negatively about him. The only other advice the aunt offers throughout the whole night is telling Abby if it was meant to be, it will be.

Before long, Abby finally reaches her bed and is fast asleep. Next morning, she jumps out of bed and speeds down to the dock with a piece of paper grasped firmly in her hand. The boatman smiles and assures Abby of her decision, raises his sails, and takes her to the other side. The boatman assures the girl the trip will be a happy one and takes her across the way.

No more than fifteen minutes pass when girl notices boy, and vice versa. They gleefully advance towards one another and share a quick embrace.

Approximately three days later, Abby wakes up and realizes her bed is colder than usual, and the boy is nowhere to be found. Shortly after this realization, she hears a thumping noise outside. She looks out the window and sees the boy chopping wood with a frustrated look on his face. She goes out and speaks with him. "Is everything okay?" The boy gives her a flat response. She warmly tells him to share with her what he is thinking. He starts mumbling and says something along the lines that things are different with her there and he is used to living alone and he feels kind of confused. Abby sort of understands where he is coming from and offers to give him a few days to ponder the situation. The boy agrees that this is a good idea. The girl and boy part ways.

As she is walking on this new side of the river, Abby runs into an old childhood school friend of hers. This boy had the biggest crush on her throughout their school years. When Abby runs into the boy she tells him how beautiful this side of the river is and they casually catch up with one another's life stories. As night is approaching, Abby informs this boy that she has no place to stay, and drops the hint that she was hoping he might be able to make room for her. To her surprise, he says no. He goes on to tell the girl that he knows the real reason she is on this side of the river and wishes not to get involved in things. She understands and bids good-bye to the boy. We do not hear from Abby again.

The first part of the story is complete. For the second part, I need you to rank each of the characters. Rank the characters using the numbers one through five, one being your favorite, and five being your least favorite. Please do this without any ties. Take your time and peruse the story again if it helps. Continue on when each person has received a number.

I tell my students this story is a "window into you." Each of the characters symbolizes something bigger, and based on how you ranked each of the people, you might learn something new about yourself. Let us look at the characters backwards in time. The second boy symbolizes pride. He knew the truth and did not want to be her second choice. Despite the encounter with his old crush, he didn't want to compromise himself. Next is the aunt. The aunt represents wisdom. She saw the boatman was taking advantage of Abby's situation. The aunt realized there is usually more than one way to get things done and tried to help her niece reach this understanding. The boatman symbolizes greed. His saw a situation that could be turned to his advantage and he did just that. Based on the numerous times I have done this story with students, the boatman is the most controversial character.

When I tell my teens Abby's story they get very passionate while defending their choices, especially with the boatman. Many of my students become convinced that the first boy and the boatman were in cahoots with each other.

The first boy the girl meets represents lust. The boy never offered to help Abby in any way, nor did he make an attempt to go to the other side, or even meet her half way. And when the boy got what he wanted from the girl, he let go of her. The last character, Abby, my favorite, symbolizes love. The girl did not let material possessions hold her back. She followed her heart and let it lead the way.

So, how did you do with Abby's story? And now that you know your results, who are you going to challenge first?

13. Mind Over Matter

Convince your students you are psychic! If your students thought you could read their minds, imagine the implications.

Here goes! Grab a piece of paper and a friend. It is best if the paper is blank on one side and has something on the other. Tear the paper into four equal parts. Tell your friend to think of a number between one and twenty-five. *When he has a number in mind, write the color black on the paper*, fold it up, and place it in a cup. Don't let your friend see what you are writing. Ask your friend what number he picked. Let's say it was ten. Now ask your friend to think of an animal. As he is thinking of an animal, you are going to write down…You've got it! Yes, you are going to write down the number ten while your partner is thinking you are writing an animal down. Continue to do this by having your partner pick a location next, and the last question you ask your partner is to pick a color, green or black. You will have a 50/50 chance of "guessing" all four correctly. Before writing down the fourth answer, pretend to have difficulty reading your friend for the answer, just in case you guessed the wrong color.

When you try this with your students, take a quick poll to see how many students believe you guessed correctly on all four (or three) attempts. Have a student take the guesses out of the cup, and watch your students fall out of their chairs.

14. Are You a Visual Learner?

I want you to picture a scientist. Try to get the most vivid description of this scientist in your head. Think of where the scientist is, what the scientist is doing, what the scientist looks like, etc…Try to think of a name for your scientist, and try to picture as many details as possible. Continue on when you are done.

When I try this activity with my students, I tell them that we are going to take a break from our regular class assignments and do a relaxing activity. I give them the same instructions, but tell them to draw what they see in their minds. After about five minutes I tell them I want them to also draw a Native American. I give them the similar descriptive instructions.

When the students appear finished, I ask them to put their markers down so they could answer the following questions. "First, raise your hand if your scientist is female. Raise your hand if your scientist appears to be inside. Raise your hand if your scientist is wearing glasses." The majority "fail" miserably at this stereotype test.

"Next, raise your hand if your Native American is wearing a feather. Raise your hand if your Native American is holding a weapon. Raise your hand if your Native American is wearing fewer clothes than your scientist."

As much as I love to do this experiment with my students, I do feel guilty for setting them up for failure. Because a valid lesson can be learned, I do this test with my students every year. Nearby, I always have examples to show my students of a female scientist working outdoors and a Native American driving a car.

On a related note, I recently purchased a four-tape set called something like the "Top 100 People of the Millennium" by A&E. It works great when you use it three people at a time, here and there. Anyhow, before using it I asked my accelerated eighth grade class who they thought made the list. To make a long story short, the first twenty people the class generated were all men. I paused after a couple moments of hearing the names and gave them the "something's wrong" look. Soon enough they read my mind and many felt awful.

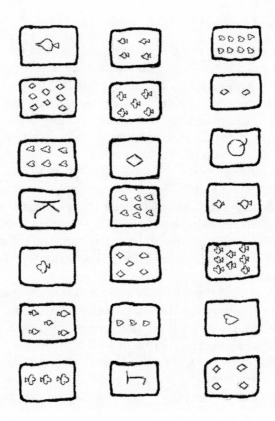

15. Make Math Magic

Ready for some math magic? Count out twenty-one cards from a standard deck of playing cards. Have the students gather around. Deal out three columns of cards, with seven cards in each. Make sure you are alternating columns. (First, put a card in column one, then two, then three, then one again, then two...) Make sure that you are putting the cards face up so that everyone can see all of the cards. Then choose a student to pick one of the cards that she sees and advise her not to tell anyone. Tell the class that by asking her only three questions, you will be able figure out her card from the twenty others. When the three columns are dealt out (all twenty-one cards) ask the student to tell you which column it is in. Without paying too much attention to the cards, neatly stack the three columns. You must make sure that you order the three stacks so that all of the cards are exactly where they started. *Whatever column the student picked goes between the other two stacks.* For instance, if she picked column C, put the stack for column C in between the stack for column A and column B. Now you are going to repeat the entire process.

Deal out the cards from the stack of twenty-one cards, first in column A, then column B, then column C, then column A again, then column B...Once again ask her which column her card is in. Stack the cards and place the column she chose in the middle of the other two stacks. Now you are going to repeat the entire process one last time. This time being the third time you go through the procedure. After the student picks the column for the third time, you know which card is her's without even looking. If you are playing along at home, you know that her card is the eleventh card from the top. What you should do next is make "flowers" with the twenty-one cards. Putting down one card at a time, face down, and counting in your head till you reach eleven, make clusters of four cards so that they look like the petals of a flower. When you make the third flower, remember where you placed the eleventh card, and without a pause deal out the rest of the cards in the same pattern of flowers.

When all of the cards are dealt out you should have five flowers, the last flower should have five petals. Now ask the student to choose two of the flowers. Here you are going to make her pick her flower petal. If the two flowers she picks has the eleventh card in them, leave them on the table and clear the rest of the cards away. If the two flowers that she picks doesn't have the card in them, clear them away. Next, ask her to pick another flower. If she picks the flower with the card, leave the flower on the table, clearing the rest. If she doesn't pick the flower with the eleventh card, clear that flower. When you have just one flower left, ask her to pick two petals. If she picks the petals with the card, leave the petals and clear the others. (I think by now you caught on to what is going on here.) No matter which flowers or petals she picks, you are going to make sure that the last card on the table is her card, the eleventh card. If all goes right, you should have the eleventh card, face down on the table. Before you allow her to pick up her card, ask her to share with the rest of the class what her card was. When she tells the rest of the class, (and be ready because sometimes they forget) ask the rest of the class to raise their hands if they think that this is her card. Now allow her to flip over the card. Viola, the ten of diamonds! Try this activity on a Friday with the students and let them figure it out over the weekend.

16. Lucky Seven

Using the following items draw a scene: Home, mountain, road, snake, sun, tree, and wallet.

This is one of those "window into your soul" activities. Whenever I do one of these activities with my students, I always state a disclaimer that reminds the students this is just an activity and they should try not to take it too seriously. I remind them that because they are in school, their pictures might not turn out the way they would if they were home. Afterwards, I also tell the students that these drawings are often used to help children, who are going through difficult stages in life, give clues to professionals that are trying to help them.

To process this activity, inform the students that each object symbolizes something larger. The home represents family, the mountain represents dreams, the road represents their timeline, the snake represents evil, the sun represents their friends, the tree represents their children, and the wallet represents money. I usually help the students with "interpreting" their drawings. I talk about how the bigger and smaller objects might relate to the importance of the symbol. The drawings in the center of the scene usually show your biggest focus. I tell them that whatever the snake is nearest is where you need to be careful of danger. If the snake is looking away from another object, that is a good sign. The location of the wallet represents their best chance to become wealthy. If their tree has a lot of fruit, that means a lot of children. If their sun has many rays, that means they have lots of friends. When the rays are all various sizes, this represents different types of friends. Lots of mountains symbolize lots of dreams. Overall, during the analysis, I remind them that I am not a professional and my insights are based on what I have read here and there. Also, I try to keep things optimistic and casual so the students don't get too emotional over the activity.

---

17. Brain Teaser

Name ten parts of the human body that are three letters long. (No slang.)

18. Multicultural Activity (Focusing on Perspective)

Harbor Master

Group size:	10-20
Age Group:	10 and up
Materials:	Blindfold
Time:	15 to 20 minutes
Location:	Large classroom or outdoors
Skills:	Cooperation, Communication, Conflict Resolution, Team Building, & Trust

a. The story behind this activity is (there should always be a story behind each activity because it makes it more enjoyable and memorable for the kids) that it's dark and the lights on shore are not working to their fullest capacity. The harbormaster has to safely bring the ship into the harbor without hitting any rocks.

b. One student will be the boat, this person is blindfolded and will start on one end of the room. (There should be a good fifteen feet between the start and finish.) The other student will start on the other side and is the harbormaster. The harbormaster is not blindfolded and she is not allowed to move into the middle area. The rest of the students are "obstacles." It is crucial that the students who act as obstacles realize that they need to be stationary and quiet.

c. To begin, have the "obstacles" take ten seconds to arrange themselves into a position that will make it challenging, but not impossible, to get the ship from the one side to the other, by following the directions of the harbormaster. After the boat makes it across, have the obstacles stay in place so that the boat can see what she went through. Process the activity when you are done.

19. Fascinating Fact

Your dominant nostril switches back and forth. (Take a deep breath through your nose. Which nostril was the strongest? Try again an hour later and see if there is a change.)

20. An Important Thing I Learned About Life is…

When you get "stressed" from life, spell that word backwards and enjoy the results.

Answer to #17—Leg, arm, eye, ear, toe, gum, lip, rib, jaw, and hip.

Chapter Three—Curriculum Enhancers

21. "The wise man doesn't give the right answers, he poses the right questions."
Claude Gustave Levi Strauss

22. My Magnum Opus

Recently it seems that competition has been likened to a four-letter word in education, and cooperation has become the magic method of success. I don't deny the immense importance of group work, but competition is part of the real world, and students need positive environments to develop the skills necessary to thrive in this arena.

The D'Amato Worksheet, as it was nicknamed by my students, is a tool that continuously gets amazing results. Before embarking on a major unit, I create a worksheet that will get them comfortable with the most challenging vocabulary words they will encounter. After they are assigned to groups of three, they compete to complete the D'Amato Worksheet by solving the Mystery Sentence. The first group to solve the Mystery Sentence wins a reward. (To figure out the Mystery Sentence, take the four letters with ones under them and *unscramble* them to find the first word. Do the same for the second word.)

Answer the following presidential trivia to simulate how the worksheet functions. (It is intentional that each answer has a different number of letters in it for practice purposes.)

(Answers: Cleveland, Clinton, Ford, Truman, Washington)

1. The only president that was a Rhodes Scholar. _ _ _ _ _ _ _
                                                              2

2. This president's mom refused to attend both his inauguration ceremonies.
_ _ _ _ _ _ _ _ _ _
    1

3. The only president not to be elected president or vice president. _ _ _ _
                                                                         2

4. The "Baby Ruth" candy bar was named after his granddaughter. _ _ _ _ _ _ _ _ _
                                                                     1 1

5. He gave the orders to drop the atomic bombs on Japan. _ _ _ _ _ _
                                                          2   1

Mystery Sentence:

_ _ _ _   _ _ _!

Completing a D'Amato Worksheet is by far my students' favorite type of regular work. They get to compete against each other and win a reward for their efforts. It takes about sixty minutes to create a worksheet and it becomes worth your time because you will wind up using it year after year. The students love the worksheet because it is a much more meaningful experience than just looking up vocabulary words in the traditional way.

Because I assign the groups, students are forced to communicate with peers they may never have talked to during the entire school year. My groupings are always based on ethnicity first. When someone enters my room, I want him/her to see a mélange of students working together. In addition to giving students opportunities to work on their social skills, it also teaches them how to work productively with others. I believe that working productively with others is one of the best work-readiness skills you can offer a student.

Lastly, I always encourage my students to think of strategies that will give them an edge over other groups. I also remind them that spelling does count. It takes students about thirty minutes to complete an average worksheet. (If a class isn't progressing fast enough, I announce the first letters of the bigger words in the Mystery Sentence as clues.) Also, I usually invite one of the members of the winning group to go over the answers in front of the room with the class. If students are slow to volunteer answers or are rude to the student, I will talk to myself aloud as I mark down points for class participation.

23. Lights, Camera, Action!!!

It is time to pantomime! Many of today's students learn best by doing. (Learning through action is often labeled kinesthetic learning.) With this in mind, can you think of a better way to have students learn/practice their vocabulary words than by acting them out?

I find pantomime most useful in connection with major units and weekly current events. At the start of a unit or before we read our current event articles, we use a D'Amato Worksheet with forty of the most challenging vocabulary words. Working on the D'Amato Worksheet allows students to familiarize themselves with the words' meanings and pronunciations. On the second day, the students review the words using pantomime.

Pantomime is simple and very high on the list of things my students love to do. Working with a partner, students act out a word, without speaking, and then call on other students to guess the word they acted out. If the first person they call on gets the answer correct, the performers *and* the guesser each receive two bonus points towards their upcoming vocabulary quiz. If the person guesses wrong, a second person may guess for one point. After two incorrect guesses, the performers must sit back down. Students do not lose points for wrong answers. (I usually have the students come up and circle the word on the list so I know which word they are performing and the other groups don't try to act out a word already done.)

Fifteen of the forty vocabulary words are ones that will be on the fill in the blank quiz at the end of the week. So when the performers indicate which word they are acting, I inform the class if it is one of our fifteen circled words or a regular word. This helps the students narrow down the possible choices for a guess.

24. How to Enjoy the Sound of Students Arguing?

Children learn best when learning is active, emotional, intellectual, and social. Only when students become excited or intrigued about the curriculum will they develop a genuine appreciation or love for learning. The Top Seven project not only achieves these goals, it also forces students to pay attention after they have made their presentation. (Too many students tune out after they present their projects in the traditional way.)

To start the Top Seven project on the Civil Rights Movement, you would first create an alphabetical list of what you (and colleagues, preferably) felt were the twenty-five most significant events that led to the success of the movement. Then, in your Media Center or as homework, students are responsible for researching twenty of the events on the list. In class you should spend some time discussing their findings. Before you assign the students to cooperative groups of three, have them make a hypothetical sequential list of what they felt were the top five events. Students should make their own list before they create a group list because that will force them to make a commitment to their choices, thus sparking more in-depth conversation and reasoning.

The students are then given time to work on, and decorate, a poster displaying the events, along with three relevant facts about each of the events they chose, to be on a separate paper. During this stage it should be suggested to the students to use the teacher as a tool. Here the teacher becomes *the guide on the side, as opposed to the sage on stage.* This is my favorite part of the unit because it allows the students to actively learn with guidance rather than passively.

For the last stage, students present their information to the rest of the class. The presentation stage becomes interactive because the groups not presenting gain or lose points based on how well they ask questions about the presentation of a group's rankings. The presenting group is also graded on how well they defend their rankings. The key here is that all groups are participating during the presentations. At the end of the project, which takes about four days, the posters are hung up with comments about their strengths and weaknesses. Because I have several classes doing this project, the posters become ideal conversation pieces between students in different period classes, which extends the learning outside the classroom.

During the project, there is a high level of excitement in the classroom, especially with the presentations. When the students start critiquing each other's posters, many of the students get very emotionally tied to their rankings. Eventually, the students realize the key is to give intellectual answers as opposed to emotional responses. The social aspect of learning plays out great here because students get to "argue" their rankings. When I started teaching, one of the first observations I made about middle school students was they love to talk their way out of anything. Years later, I have finally found a way to enjoy the sound of adolescents arguing.

25. In Full Bloom

What is the most important tool a teacher has access to? Many will say the Internet. While it is an invaluable tool for students, I happen to believe the Internet is the most poorly, most misused tool available. I personally believe Bloom's Taxonomy is by far the most valuable tool at a teacher's disposal.

The way in which I use the taxonomy most is for homework assignments. Instead of using the textbook questions at the end of a section, which happens to be what students list as their least favorite part of a textbook, I allow the students to come up with six of their own questions, which they will in turn answer. Students will create one question per category from Bloom's taxonomy using a key word as a question starter.

1. Knowledge—Choose, collect, define, label, list, match, name, outline, quote, rephrase, show, tell, when, where, which, or who.

2. Comprehension—Associate, classify, compare, contrast, describe, differentiate, discuss, distinguish, estimate, extend, interpret, predict, relate, summarize, or why.

3. Application—Apply, build, calculate, change, construct, demonstrate, discover, examine, identify, illustrate, modify, relate, select, show, or solve.

4. Analysis—Analyze, assume, categorize, conclude, connect, explain, infer, order, separate, or simplify.

5. Synthesis—Adapt, change, combine, compose, create, design, develop, elaborate, generalize, imagine, improve, integrate, plan, predict, propose, rearrange, substitute, suppose, or "what if."

6. Evaluation—Assess, convince, criticize, decide, discriminate, evaluate, judge, justify, measure, prove, recommend, support, test, or value.

26. Size Does Matter

Never underestimate the power of poster paper. Poster paper is always the first thing I order when the supply lists come around at the end of the year. For whatever reason, the bigger the paper the students do their work on, the more motivated they become. I figure a big piece of poster paper allows for more creativity. In the end, the posters come out great and the students become much more concerned with grammar and spelling than usual.

27. Don't be a Bore

Take time to find interesting ways to review. Buy a beach ball and throw it to students instead of calling on them. Try a Starburst candy review. If there is one thing that can get an apathetic class to do "flips," it is candy. Five dollars here and there goes a long way. (Or you can go overboard and buy your classes $470 worth of gourmet Belgian chocolate while on holiday in Brussels.) As for spending money on students, I have heard the average teacher spends over three hundred dollars a year on stuff for the class. The way I see it, I am simply donating to my favorite charity. (Oh, if you save your receipts, you can claim your purchases during tax season.)

28. ABC, as Easy as 1, 2, 3

Do you remember partaking in a scavenger hunt when you were younger? During the summer, my campers had to obtain things like socks, hair from a counselor, five hugs, a silly joke, etc…They were fun times!

For this classroom scavenger hunt, I first get the students to write the letters A through Z on a poster paper. (Thirteen letters on one side, and the other thirteen down the middle.) I also ask them to think of a team name and write it at the top of the paper. Choosing a team name creates more of a commitment to the assignment. Next, I will give them a topic and tell them the group that finds the most words beginning with each letter of the alphabet, in seven minutes, wins a reward. (When using poster paper, it is best to give the students several colored markers so they can express their creativity.)

Sample topic: Harlem Renaissance

A—Apollo Theatre   B—Baldwin, James
C—Cotton Club   D—(Great) Depression
E—Ellington, Duke   F—Fearless

29. Saved By the Bell

Students have different learning styles. Some prefer audio over visual. Some prefer writing over reading. And some prefer running across the room, smacking a bell, and shouting an answer that will help their team win. I believe that learning is most memorable when it is exciting.

For this activity you need to make a list of questions, mostly review, and then create two teams. Mark a starting line on one side of the classroom, and put two bells on top of a desk on the opposite side. (Leave about ten feet between the start and end.) Put the names of all the members in the first group in a cup, and do the same for the second group in a different cup. Call one name from each side to line up. Tell them they could cross the line whenever they are ready to answer the question. Begin reading the question and stop when the first person crosses the line. A correct answer gets a team two points. If the first person rings, and gets it wrong, the other team's person can earn double the points for a right answer. If one team is winning by a lot, I will increase the point value of the questions to keep both teams focused on the activity.

30. Character Development

How would you go about introducing a famous person or event? I would start with a graphic organizer called a KWL chart. (A KWL chart has three equal columns that take up an entire page.) The KWL chart helps students organize information into three categories: What they **Know**, what they **Want** to know, and what they **Learned**. I love using the question, "What do we already know about…" to get things started.

To dive into Dr. Martin Luther King, Jr.'s birthday, my students use a KWL chart. (In preparation for the lesson, I create a list of ten relevant facts about Dr. King I want the students to discuss.) For an anticipatory set, I usually ask the students, "Who is the only person born in the U.S.A. to have his/her own national holiday?" They all tend to guess correctly because of when we do the lesson. Next, I use the KWL chart like a "Think, Pair, and Share" activity. I tell them to *think* of facts from television, books, or from people that they remember about Dr. King. They are instructed to record this information in the "Know" column. After a few minutes they are instructed to discuss their findings in *pairs* and record any new information in the "Learned" column. After a couple of minutes, students are asked to think of questions they have about Dr. King and write them in the "Want" column. After the writing part we discuss or *share* our findings. If I tell them they could use these notes for a few minutes on the upcoming test, it increases the productivity of the lesson. I use the KWL charts with each new major theme/unit.

31. A Picture is Worth a Thousand Words

When introducing a new unit, find a picture or two that encapsulates the event or time period. When my students are doing an analysis of an artwork or photograph I give them a worksheet and use the "Think, Pair, and Share" format. Our discussions during these lessons are the most impressive throughout the entire year.

The following seven questions are the guiding questions that we use to analyze the artwork/pictures:

What do you see?

What do you notice about the people in the picture?

Where do you think the people are?

What is the mood in the picture? Elaborate.

From looking at the artwork/photograph, what can you tell about the artist?

What message do you believe the artist wanted to send with this picture?

If you were to give this piece a title, what would it be? Elaborate.

32. To Bee or Not to Bee

Students love bees! To review for our final exam at the end of the year we have a category bee. They have seven categories to choose from: Age of Exploration, Colonial America, U.S. Civil War, Civil Rights Movement, etc…Then participating students are each given names and events that they must place in the correct category to continue. The categories bee runs just like a regular spelling bee and can be used in almost every class.

For those who still feel that competition should not be in the classroom, life for most of our students will only be getting more and more competitive each year. They need to know how to handle the ups and downs that come with competing.

33. Chutes and Ladders

Reviewing for rewards. An interesting way to review past people, places, or events is to use the ladder technique. Using an overhead projector, reveal information about a proper noun, one clue at a time. Tell the students they only get one guess per puzzle and there is no penalty for an incorrect guess, aside from being out of that round. I reward the winners with prizes.

(ex.) Western Hemisphere / Provinces / Territories / Ottawa / Hockey Hall of Fame / Niagara Falls

34. Brain Teaser

What is the most deadly creature in the world?

35. Multicultural Activity (Focusing on Distractions)

<u>Pass Around</u>

Group size: 7-20
Age Group: 8 and up
Materials: Small objects, like balls, that can be tossed around
Time: 15 to 20 minutes
Location: Classroom or outdoors
Skills: Multicultural Appreciation, Perspective, Focusing, & Fun

a. Have everyone stand in a circle. Get a person to start with the ball and have her pass it to someone else, preferably someone not to her immediate left or right.

b. Have the students keep passing it around until everyone touches it once. Make sure no student gets it twice. At some point, remind them to remember who they threw it to.

c. After the first round where everyone touched it once, have them do it again to make sure they are comfortable with the rhythm. Now here comes the interesting/challenging part, add another ball each time they successfully complete the sequence. In other words, start with two students having balls, passing in the same progression after they master one ball without dropping it. Then give three students a ball each when they master two balls in the same progression. (Quick tip: The student will always receive the ball from the same person and the student will always send the ball to the same student.)

d. Process the activity: What was the hardest part of the activity? What does this activity have to do with school/life?

36. Fascinating Facts

There are currently about 27 million slaves in the world. (According to the U.S. Department of State, over a hundred nations annually have at least a hundred people who are "bought and sold, held captive, and exploited for profit," including the U.S.A.)

37. An Important Thing I Learned About Life is...

Don't be the first to let go of a hug.

Answer to #33—Canada

Answer to #34—Mosquitoes kill over one million people a year, spreading diseases like malaria and the West Nile virus. If you guessed a human, that was my first guess too.

Chapter Four—Discipline

38. "Yelling is what teachers do when they run out of intelligent things to say."
Michael James D'Amato

39. Stupid is as Stupid Does

The million dollar question for teachers: Why do students misbehave? For many chronic misbehavers, these students would simply rather look tough than stupid. To learn more about students who misbehave frequently, notice *when* they act up. Many of the times it will happen when they are faced with a task which makes them feel inadequate.

40. Big Brother is Watching

When disciplining a student, pretend her mother is in the room. This strategy should help you focus and be articulate.

41. Are You and Your Students Seeing Eye to Eye?

Talk with students at eye level when disciplining. When I know that a student is having big problems, I get down to her level, literally. On the other hand, you have the "cat in the corner" scenario: Some teachers like to tower over their students and show them who the boss is.

Despite the very firm, concrete, and sometimes cold philosophy I follow, that side of me lasts for at most the "first fifteen days." Once I have the class in a rhythm that works, which in recent years takes less than a week, I consider myself to be a very sympathetic and sensitive teacher.

42. Document, Document, Document

I've heard the three key words in real estate are location, location, location. With that in mind, the three key words when dealing with a challenging student have to be document, document, and document. If there is a student who is really pushing your buttons, and you have already talked to your colleagues about her, the next step is to keep a log of all the specific things she is doing wrong in class. It is probably a good idea to also list the times and dates.

Keeping a record of her misbehaviors falls under the "CYA" approach to managing your affairs. (Covering Your Assets.)

43. Oreos

If you are like me and sometimes feel uncomfortable giving the adult of a student bad news, mix it in between two positive comments. I think part of my issue is that I don't have any children of my own. For that reason, I sometimes feel awkward giving advice about parenting.

On a related note, when we have an adult come in about a challenging student, the guidance department usually "oreos" me between two firmer teachers so I don't confuse the adult with my sensitive nature. (We all get a good laugh over it every time it happens.)

44. Feeling Blue?

Have special blue hall passes for those times when you need a student to leave and have someone hold/watch her for you till the end of the period. (The blue pass serves as a code between you and another teacher.)

45. Bank Withdrawls

We all have our breaking points. Some days it seems like every student has an issue with something. On days like these it is good to have a backup word, or bank of words if you are that…creative. For me the term is "shut up." When things seem uncontrollable and I don't have anything left in the gas tank, I have reserved that term to be my wakeup call.

46. The Early Bird

Penalize students who flip their tests over early, call out answers, or whisper answers to their neighbors. It is a bad habit that needs to be extinguished before your students move on to the next level of their education. (When you grade papers, use a marker, but not a red one, because you can tell if they erased a wrong answer and tried to make it right.)

47. Criticize the Behavior, Not the Person

When you must correct a student's actions, teachers are supposed to criticize bad behavior or bad choices. Never send the message the student is bad.

48. Brain Teaser

What creature moves on four legs in the morning, two in the afternoon, and three at night?

49. Multicultural Activity (Focusing on Connectedness)

Tangled Together

Group size:	10-25
Age Group:	10 and up
Materials:	A piece of paper with the numbers 1 to 100 written on it.
Time:	20 to 30 minutes

Location: Classroom
Skills: Multicultural Appreciation, Cooperation, Trust, & Conflict
                Resolution

The following activity was taught to me by a student who learnt it while studying in the Middle East. I use this activity before a major unit on that area of the world. The students love it. (The day before the activity you might want to mention to your students they should wear comfortable clothes because they will be moving around. Tell them to avoid any clothes they wouldn't wear playing Twister.)

a. When you are ready to begin have the students form a circle. To start this activity, have a piece of paper with the numbers one through four times the number of students you have. (If you have twenty students, the list should be from one to eighty.) Then assign each student four numbers. (Since the four numbers are consecutive, the students only really need to remember one number.) Go around the circle and give out the four numbers for each student. The four numbers that you are going to give out goes as follows: One for her right hand, two for her left hand, three for her right foot, and four for her left foot. The next student gets five, six, seven, and eight. Do this till everyone has four numbers.

b. After everyone has a number, ask the group, on the count of three, to count off their numbers and stick out the appropriate body part. This procedure is a decent way to make sure that everyone is ready to move on. It is also a good way to give the students an opportunity to get a little silly, because what they are going to do next is going to require them to be flexible within their comfort zones.

c. Now the teacher reads off two numbers. The two numbers should not be within five of each other. If you call out 19 and 38, then the students with these numbers go inside the circle and join their 19 and 38 body parts. If 19 is someone's right foot and 38 is someone's left hand, they have to connect them. These two body parts have to remain connected until the end of the activity.

d. After each successful connection, call off another two numbers. Make sure you are crossing off the numbers as you go. It may also be a good idea to circle the number and then cross it off after they are definitely joined. Try to get the class to complete the entire list of numbers. The larger the group, the harder the task. It might be a good idea to do a countdown stating how many pairs are left as they go on. This way they know the finish line is near. Students may move around to fit the next match, but they should remain connected at all times. If the connection breaks, make sure they reconnect. Be prepared to have fun and laugh!

e. Process the activity: Was this activity difficult for you in the beginning? Why didn't you give up?

50. Fascinating Fact

One million earths could fit inside the sun.

51. An Important Thing I Learned About Life is…

If you feel you are about to be attacked, don't yell help, yell fire.

Answer to #48—Human—As a baby, in the morning, she crawls on all four, during the middle years she walks upright on two legs, and in her late years she walks with a cane, on three legs.

Chapter Five—Classroom Management

52. "Good teaching is one-fourth preparation and three-fourths theater." Gail Godwin

53. The Ripple Effect

There are two constants I have noticed about children over the years: They are constantly comparing themselves to their peers and they want their teacher to like them. One of the psychological strategies I like to use to speed things up when making a transition is to say something positive about the students who have already started the next assignment. For example, "I really like how Chris and Diana have already taken out their notebooks and started answering the first problem." Statements like this tend to send ripples through the class.

Another way to use the ripple effect when students are taking too long to make a transition, or get ready, is to start counting down from ten. "10, 9, 8, 7…" It amazes me how well this technique works, even with teenagers.

54. My Fair Lady

Being fair simply means being consistent. Your rules/policies need to apply to all students, all of the time. If you don't accept late homework, you never accept late homework. If you don't let students go to their lockers, there can be no exceptions. Well, asthmatic reasons and other emergencies should be respected. If your students start to see you as unfair, or showing favoritism, they will lose a lot of respect for you. Remember, respect begets respect. No exceptions.

With respect to favoritism, it always makes me laugh when I hear a teacher say he has no favorites. Let's be real, we are human. It is natural to have favorites, but it is unwise to make it known.

55. What Would Grandma Do?

Grandma saves the best things for last. My grandmother would always have the best desserts out, but you couldn't get a taste until you finished your vegetables. If you do have a snack, surprise, or activity for your students, make sure you get through the curriculum work first, before the treat.

56. Are You the Quiet Type?

What is the best way to get shy students to participate in class? Build their confidence up with easier questions. Many of them want to participate, but are fearful, and their reasons are valid.

57. Twist and Shout

For the student who constantly turns around and talks, tell her to put her knees under her desk.

---

58. Brain Teaser

Jason was born on January 16th, yet his birthday is always in the summer. How is this possible?

59. Multicultural Activity (Focusing on Group Dynamics)

Electric Fence

Group size:	8-20
Age Group:	10 and up
Materials:	Rope/string and gymnasium mats
Time:	15 to 20 minutes
Location:	Large classroom or outdoors
Skills:	Multicultural Appreciation, Cooperation, Trust, Conflict Resolution, & Team Building

a. Set up an area where a rope, slightly above waist high, serves as the top of an electric fence. Place gym mats on both sides for safety purposes. The rope could be tied between two chairs. There should be about eight feet of rope between the chairs.

b. Your students are to start on one side of the fence and they have to get everybody over to the other side without touching the electric fence. (Ouch!)

c. Despite its difficulty and the slight danger involved, (I would never recommend an activity that I had someone get hurt while participating) it is a really great team-building activity. Occasionally, I will add a blindfold or make someone mute to enhance the challenge.

d. Process the activity: What was the hardest part of the activity? Did you have doubts? What were the biggest problems that your group faced? Did you want to give up?

60. Fascinating Fact

Those who died while building the Great Wall of China were conveniently placed inside it.

61. An Important Thing I Learned About Life is…

Enjoy every sandwich.

Answer to #58—Jason lives in the Southern Hemisphere where the seasons are opposite those in the Northern Hemisphere.

Chapter Six—Student Rapport

62. "A student won't care how much you know, until he knows how much you care." Jaime Escalante

63. Let Them Cheat?

Allow your students to use notes for five minutes of a test. This idea is worth trying at least once just to experience the frantic flapping of pages and shuffling of books that happen the moment you say, "Alright, you now have five minutes of open notes."

The main rules I give to students are they can't use the textbook, someone else's notes, or photocopies of notes. Allowing them to use their notes reduces the potential of cheating and eventually will make them more organized. It also gives you an excuse to avoid the annoying and time-consuming notebook checks. Last but not least, it gives you a legitimate answer to the question: Why do we take notes?

64. Let Me Hear Your Body Talk

93% of communication is nonverbal. Often it is not what you say, but how you say it. Many teachers have very loud nonverbal language and don't realize it.

65. Show Me the Money

Very few teachers use immediate concrete reinforcements for positive actions. One can only expect verbal praise to motivate students so much. It is obvious the more immediate and worthwhile the reinforcement, the better the responses.

My students can earn D'Amato Dollars when they work extra hard, do something extraordinary, or solve a D'Amato Worksheet. Three dollars can buy them a homework pass, school supplies, or fifteen points on an upcoming test. During the fourth marking period, a dollar can buy them a lollipop. These dollars help create a classroom where being smart, participating, and taking risks are positive behaviors.

For those of you who get really nervous when being observed by your supervisor or principal, "dollars" are a great way to get the students engaged if you are doing a regular lesson and someone pops in to evaluate you. There is nothing wrong with using the dollars as a crutch when they pop in. At least that is what I tell myself after each time it happens.

66. Going Clubbing

Get to know your students outside the classroom. Any solid relationship involves both give and take. Show students that you are interested in their lives outside your classroom and they should perform better in your classroom.

Getting involved in clubs or attending their extracurricular activities is also a fantastic way to get feedback from your students. In addition, it will give you a better picture of your students. I have been surprised countless times to see students who are angels in the classroom act like clowns in the hall. If you only know one side of a student's personality you are limiting yourself in how you could help her grow. Most importantly, making an effort outside the classroom shows your students you are human. Kind of like when they see you in the food store and they give you that bizarre look that says, "You shop for food?"

67. Are You a Doormat?

What message do you send your students as they enter the classroom? In the beginning of the year, I stick to the "first fifteen days" rule and remain distant and strict. However, once I know I have a level of control I am comfortable with, I offer a warm welcome to all my students. I want my students to know I am glad they are part of the class. We should also make sure to show them we want to be there too. This means not counting the days till the end of summer. Children are very perceptive. They know who wants to be there and who doesn't.

---

68. Brain Teaser

A woman shoots a man. Then she submerges him under water for several minutes. Finally, she hangs him. Half an hour later the woman and the man go out and enjoy a romantic dinner. How is this possible?

69. Multicultural Activity (Focusing on Discipline)

<u>Dragon's Lair</u>

Group size:	8-20
Age Group:	7 and up
Materials:	Ball or something easy to grab
Time:	10 to 15 minutes
Location:	Large classroom or outdoors
Skills:	Cooperation, Communication, Conflic Resolution, & Team Building

a. Have students form a large circle by joining hands. Explain that there is a dragon that protects the most expensive jewels in the world and you have been selected to steal them from the dragon. If the dragon touches you once, you become frozen and are eliminated from the round.

b. Choose one person to start in the middle with the jewels under her legs. (The dragon should not touch the jewels to protect them.) Tell the dragon to roar when she is ready. Once she roars, all of the others are against her and have to steal her jewels without being frozen.

c. This is one of those activities where you need to have eyes in the back of your head. It is a very fun and playful activity.

d. Process the activity: Which role was more difficult? How can you relate this activity to school?

70. Fascinating Fact

In 1980, the city of Detroit, Michigan, presented Saddam Hussein with a key to the city.

71. An Important Thing I Learned About Life is…

Never let money clog your artery of life.

Answer to #68—The woman is a photographer.

Chapter Seven—Potent Phrases

72. "Teach today, touch tomorrow." Anonymous

73. We are Family

Do all of your students have parents? That is not the norm where I teach. When sending a note home, or addressing the class, please don't tell students to have their parents sign the paper. Use families, it is a much safer word.

74. What are a Teacher's Three Greatest Words?

June, July, and August, right? Alas, there are three that are even more wonderful. "Remind me later." Think about it, throughout the school day you will be asked hundreds of questions or favors from students and other teachers. You can't afford to be burdened with all these trivial things. So give them back to their owners.

The next time a student asks you for an extra credit assignment on the last day of a marking period, simply reply with your new favorite words and you won't have to feel guilty about forgetting.

On a side note about summer vacation, I run into many teachers who live by the "half a day, half a year" mentality of why teaching is great. Reality check, most teachers in France and other European countries teach about eighteen hours a week. A French friend of mine was promoted last summer and he went from eighteen to fifteen hours of class time a week. The main difference is they are allotted about the same amount of hours in preparation/meeting time. And yes, their salaries are pretty much the same as ours. C'est la vie!

75. Ask Three, Then Me

One of my biggest missions as a teacher is to foster independence in my students. Many of our students rely on teachers for the most trivial things. This is not a good habit. Get your students to ask three students their question before asking you and you have fostered a positive habit they will use for the rest of their lives.

76. What are you Waiting for?

"Waiting is not working!" This line is the most recent addition to my common classroom sayings. Many of our students are under the impression that not working is a valid option. Whether they are waiting for glue, a computer, or the dismissal bell to ring, they always need to have work out. (As you may have guessed, they get a concrete punishment when they are waiting and not working.) Be careful, there is one exception to this expression, and that is when students reply, "I'm thinking."

77. Fight, Flight, or Freeze

Do you teach life lessons? I am not exactly sure why I decided to include my little life lessons at the end of each chapter. It is possible that I wanted to share a little bit more about myself. Or maybe it was the hope that a few of my past students might one day come across this book and see one of the ideas and think back to our times together.

One of the most important things our students need to learn about is dealing with conflict. Our students, especially teenagers, are faced with some sort of conflict on a regular basis. To help students deal with their conflicts, I like to offer the fight, flight, or freeze model. Basically, when confronted with any conflict, one has three main choices, one of the three F's. Students who know their options in a conflict tend to deal with it better.

78. Does This Count?

"This will be graded." If you notice that some students are not putting enough effort into an assignment, mention to the class it will be graded and it should get most of them back on track.

79. R U P C?

Do you remember sitting Indian style when you were younger? The world is becoming more and more politically correct every day, especially so in schools. As a teacher/role model, you need to set the example for your students. Nowadays, *guys and girls* should be sitting like "pretzels."

80. You Can't Make Me

Sometimes students don't want to be bothered. As teachers we need to offer the option to pass, but in a way in which the student won't take advantage of this privilege. If a student doesn't want to work on a particular assignment, you must give a quick and clear consequence so the other students know passing on an assignment is never in their best interest. If it is an important assignment and you get the attitude, casually remind the students that it is worth a large percent of their average.

When it comes to participating in activities, I like to use the term "challenge by choice" with the students. If a particular activity is not something they are comfortable with, then they have the option to sit out. It is important to note that sitting out doesn't mean they talk with a friend the whole period or do something more interesting. At the very least, it should mean the student sits out by herself, just watching. If the student gets to sit out and do whatever she wants, then others will want the same thing.

81. Are We Having Fun Yet?

Do your students earn fun days? Students definitely need to be rewarded for their efforts. However, I would suggest that those who have "Fun Days" or "Fun Friday" reconsider their options. (Think semantics.) Maybe "Specialty Day" is more appropriate. Terms like "Fun Day" get around quickly, and chances are they will catch the ear of your principal or a concerned parent.

---

82. Brain Teaser

Randomly gather one hundred quarters, what are the odds (percentage) that you have a U.S. quarter from 1975?

83. Multicultural Activity (Focusing on Strategizing)

Everybody's it

Group size:	10-25
Age Group:	7 and up
Materials:	None
Time:	15 to 20 minutes
Location:	Outdoors or gymnasium
Skills:	Fun

a. This is a tag game where everybody is it and the last one standing is the winner.

b. Anyone can get anyone else out. The way to get someone out is to tag them without them tagging you. If two people tag each other at the same time, neither is out, and there is a five-second period where both have to wait if they want to tag each other again. As a teacher you need to watch the students carefully on this one because there will be many disagreements. When it comes to activities like this one, I always take a proactive approach and tell my students before we start that I am the only referee here and even though I am not perfect, I make the final calls.

c. Process the activity: What was the most challenging part of the activity? Did you have any strategies or make any alliances?

84. Fascinating Fact

Time's "Man of the Year" in 1938 was Adolf Hitler.

85. An Important Thing I Learned About Life is…

Quickest way to feel younger: Climb a fence.

Answer to #82—Zero. There were no quarters made in 1975 due to the preparation of the 1976 bicentennial quarter.

Chapter Eight—Perplexing Puzzles

86. "Too often we give our children answers to remember, rather than problems to solve." Roger Lewin

87. As Thick as Thieves

Here is the situation: Person A has a chest, key A, and lock A. Person B has a diamond, key B, and lock B. Key A only works with lock A and key B only works with lock B. Person A is on the top and Person B is on the bottom. Both people are always stationary. Between the two people is a thief. (Mentioning that she is a billion dollar thief usually comes in handy when the students try to come up with sneaky ways of shifting objects between Person A and Person B.) Person B has to get his diamond in the hands of person A without the thief stealing it. Between Person A and Person B is a conveyor belt that things can be passed back and forth. However, each time something is passed back and forth, the thief will check to see if she wants it. If the box is passed across and it is locked, the thief will not steal it. If the box is passed and it is unlocked, she will steal whatever is inside. However, she will not steal the empty box. If a key, lock, or the diamond is passed on the conveyor belt, she will steal it, unless it is locked in the box. Anything passed must be on the conveyor belt. There are no bizarre tricks needed to solve this problem. Students will try to think of tricks like throwing things or hiding pieces. When Person A has the diamond in his hand, the puzzle is complete.

This puzzle is fun and educational! (The person who shared this puzzle with me said it had to do with computers and encryption. The students won't need this knowledge to solve the puzzle.) Every class I have done this puzzle with was engaged the entire time and the students always clapped for the person who eventually solved the puzzle. (When the students are sharing ideas aloud, it usually takes about ten minutes for someone in the class to finally solve it.) It is an amazing thing to see the students attack this one.

(Here is a quick hint: The puzzle can be solved in four moves.)

88. Ummmm...

For this activity, students will try to guess a word that fits a pattern. The pattern for this activity is the person says "Ummm" before the word. For example, "Ummm, turtle" is acceptable, but "turtle" is not. It sounds dull, but this one really gets them excited.

89. Have a Ball!

If you want to reward your class with a quick activity, try this one. For this activity, you only need a ball or something you can pass around. Inform the students you have a ball and will pass it around the room and then hide it under someone's chair. Tell them that you are going to hide it under someone's chair so fast they won't even see it. To start, pass the ball to a student, have her pass it to someone else, and so on, until about four students touched the ball. After the last student touches the ball, it gets passed back to you. When you get the ball back, make sure they are quiet at this time, then ask the question,

"Under whose chair was the ball?" (You want students to call out and not raise their hands.) After a few have guessed, tell them where you "hid" the ball. The solution to this quandary is the person whose chair it was under was the person who spoke first after you asked the question, "Under whose chair was the ball?" Because it is a difficult activity, you might want to give clues as you go along, such as asking them which senses they are relying on to solve the puzzle. If they are not catching on, I will usually tell them to close their eyes and try to figure out the solution.

90. Two Guys and a Girl

There are two guys and a girl on one side of a lake and they all need to get to the other side of the lake. The two guys weigh exactly 75 pounds each and the female weighs 90 pounds. The boat can hold no more than 150 pounds at a time and their entire bodies must be in the boat at all times. (Let us say there are piranhas in the water.) Figure out a way to get all three people to the other side safely.

91. Count Me In

For this activity, let's say you have twenty students in your class. The goal of this activity is to have your students count to twenty in a way that each person can only say a number once. The students can't speak unless it is a number and when more than one person says a number at a time, you start over. This game is cute and always brings out a good laugh. One thing you should state in the directions is that you are going to bark at anyone who says something other than a number. You will need to bark because some students will try to talk to organize the group. In the end, they will need to use nonverbal communication to solve this challenge.

92. Green Glass Mirror

Write the words "green glass mirror" on the chalkboard. Invite your students to walk through the green glass mirror, figuratively. Tell them in order to successfully walk through the mirror, they need to carry something "appropriate." The pattern the students need to figure out in order to walk through the mirror is they need to bring something that has double letters. (Green, Glass, Mirror = EE, SS, RR)

A similar version is called "Around the World." Students have to name a place and you tell them whether they can go with you on the trip or not. The students have to figure out the particular pattern. Sample patterns could be: All places could have two syllables, begin with the same first letter as the person who is guessing, or a place located in Africa.

93. Happy Birthday

Here is a quick conflict resolution activity dealing with nonverbal communication. First, tell them they may not talk during the entire activity. (Stress the no-talking rule several times.) Then tell your students they will have three minutes, or more depending on the size of your class, to line up in birthday order, not including year. In order to complete this challenge, the entire class needs to be in order from January 1st to December 31st. I played this activity with people from Europe the first time and since they put the day first, then the month (Pearl Harbor Day was on 7/12/41 for them) it created a chaotic, but fun mess.

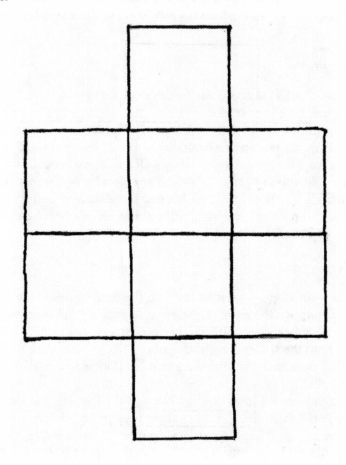

94. Eight is Enough

Place the numbers one through eight in the boxes so that no two consecutive numbers touch each other horizontally, vertically, or diagonally.

---

95. Brain Teaser

What comes next? O, T, T, F, F, S, S,?,?,?

96. Multicultural Activity (Focusing on Inner Strength)

<u>Hypotheticals</u>

Group size:	10-25
Age Group:	10 and up
Materials:	None
Time:	15 to 20 minutes
Location:	Classroom or outdoors
Skills:	Multicultural Appreciation & Perspective

a. For this activity, you will need to designate two sides in your classroom. You will also need to come up with a list of hypothetical or current event questions for the students to answer. You will ask a question like, "Did the U.S. do the right thing by dropping atomic bombs on Japan?" "Would you cheat on the final exam if your friend had a copy?" "Do you think China's one-child policy is a smart idea?"

b. After you ask the question, direct the students to the left for the first option and to the right for the other. (I always allow a middle ground for the students to use.) Ask for volunteers to explain their answers. By setting up the room this way and allowing the students to move around and stand, they may be more comfortable sharing their reasoning.

c. Process this activity: Did your stance on any issue change? Is peer pressure always bad?

97. Fascinating Fact

Right after the Taj Mahal was built, the architect's eyes were gouged out so he could never build anything as beautiful again.

98. An Important Thing I Learned About Life is...

Take hugs daily as if they were vitamins.

Answer to #87—Person A sends the empty box down. Person B puts the diamond in the box, locks it, and sends it across. Person A <u>double locks</u> the box with his lock and sends it back down. Person B removes his lock with his key and then sends the box up, leaving Person A's lock still on the box. Person A removes his lock with his key and then removes the diamond.

Answer to #90—Both 75's go over and one comes back. Then 90 goes over and 75 comes back. Then both 75's go back over.

Answer to #94   3 5
                  7 1 8 2
                     4 6

Answer to #95—E, N, T. Eight, Nine, and Ten.

Chapter Nine—Intangibles

99. "Teaching is essential to my life." Elie Wiesel

100. What's Worse Than Death?

Want to create chemistry in your class? Have the students come up with three stories for homework. One will be a true story about their past, and the other two will be fictional. After they read their stories in front of the class, it becomes an activity for the students to guess which story was real.

As teachers, we sometimes forget how difficult it is for people to speak in front of a group. I once read people rank public speaking as their biggest fear, slightly above death.

101. A Key to Life

What drives you? The three things that dictate how I live my life are the quest for knowledge, helping others, and being somewhere new. Each of these things has one major thing in common, anticipation. Like many people, I sometimes enjoy the anticipation of what I look forward to doing more than the act itself. Our anticipation of an event often gives us a rush. With this thought in mine, before you go to sleep tonight, find one thing to look forward to tomorrow. Waking up and commuting to work should become much more interesting.

On a related note, it is not that I hate doing dishes, it is the anticipation of doing them that annoys me.

102. I Think We're Alone Now

Never be alone with just one student. If you find you are, make sure your door is open, and either stand at the door or invite another teacher/student over. If you have to be in the classroom, sit behind your desk to create a barrier from the student. This may seem extreme, but I would rather sound overly paranoid than to have the education system lose a quality teacher because of someone's overactive imagination. This situation happens most often after school. Oh, and I don't care if there is a hurricane, never give a student a ride home.

103. Don't Worry, Be Happy

Avoid telling students not to worry. If a student happens to bring her problems to school, you may have seen it happen before, telling her not to worry may cause her to not trust her feelings, her gut. A better approach might be to validate her feelings by saying it is *normal* to worry about some things. For example, if a family member is late picking up Suzy, let her know it is natural for her to be concerned.

104. Can You Keep a Secret?

Don't make promises and never swear to keep a secret. I doubt that I need to elaborate here.

105. The Envelope Please

Want to really let a student know she is doing great? Type a letter to her family and share with them what it is she does in the classroom that separates her from the average student. Pour your heart into it. Place the letter in the envelope and *don't* seal it. Chances are her curiosity will get the best of her before the day is over.

106. Music Soothes the Savage Beast

Music is one of the most powerful forces known to humans. Very few things could change a person's mood as quickly and drastically as a song. I have even heard arguments that listening to classical music before a test increases performance. I doubt that is the case, but I do know when I pop in some Beethoven or Mozart while my students are working on a D'Amato Worksheet they recognize the tunes quickly, and some even hum along to the songs. I was being observed by my supervisor on one occasion and I received a compliment on my evaluation sheet about Ravel Bolero in the background.

I have also been told that of all the scents out there, vanilla is the most relaxing. Before you rush out to buy candles in bulk, they do make scented sprays, and I have seen fair results.

In addition, I have read that peppermint stimulates the brain. Therefore, it has become a tradition for me to hand out mint candies on test days to increase the students' mental sharpness.

107. Be All You Can Be

Who are you while teaching? Early in my career I reached the conclusion I would have to adjust my personality if I wanted to survive as a teacher. Being soft-spoken, I thought only a mean teacher could get things done and that would lead me to become stern and miserable. At first, that was exactly what happened. I went home and those closest to me learned to stay away.

After two years, I gained control over my classes by adopting a few new theories about teaching (all conveniently listed in this book) and I finally learned how to be myself in front of the students. Now I look forward to coming to school every day where I can be myself and get positive results.

108. Culture Club

Can we teach culture? That's debatable. We can most definitely *expose* them to it on a regular basis. I always thought the best teachers were those who let you explore their world. Whether they brought in brochures, trinkets, photos, or stories from a recent trip, I always wanted to be the teacher who lived, and loved, life.

Do you value teaching your students culture? Ponder the following question and you will have your answer: How often do you think about your students when you are in a gift shop in a foreign place?

109. Donkey Who?

Don Quixote de la Mancha. It may have taken ten renditions of "Dulcinea" and a few too many tilts at invisible windmills, but I can assure you none of my students will ever forget the name Miguel de Cervantes. We are all passionate about something. If you love something, share it. Passion cannot be faked, and it is hard to forget. Don Quixote might not be part of my curriculum, but it has been voted the greatest novel of all time on several occasions. Therefore, it is relevant, and I don't need any other reason to bring it up every year. If you can be openly passionate about something in front of your students, that may be one of the greatest compliments you can give yourself.

110. Brain Teaser

Here is the scenario: There is a dead guy with four bullet wounds, he is in his car, all the doors are locked from the inside, and all the windows are up. There is no gun in the car. There is no damage to the car. How did he die?

111. Multicultural Activity (Focusing on Plain Old Fun)

<u>Squirrels</u>

Group size:	10-25
Age Group:	10 and up
Materials:	Balloons
Time:	15 to 20 minutes
Location:	Large classroom or outdoors
Skills:	Communication, Conflict Resolution, & Fun

a. Tell a story about how squirrels collect nuts for the winter. "Today we have a greedy group that didn't store enough food." Give each student a balloon (nuts) to place between their legs.

b. Your objective is to steal the nuts of the other squirrels by breaking their balloons. Students cannot attack someone else's balloon unless their balloon is between their legs. (This rule is important for safety purposes.) Students are not allowed to keep their hands on the balloons.

c. If a student drops her balloon, she can go and get it if no one pops it before it is reached. Last squirrel standing wins.

d. Process the activity: What was the most difficult part of the challenge? What would you do differently if we were to try it again?

112. Fascination Fact

Alaska has over three million lakes.

113. An Important Thing I Learned About Life is...

The sun shines for all.

Answer to #110—The guy is in a convertible.

Chapter Ten—The Fifteen Most Common Mistakes Made by Teachers Today.

114. "It's your attitude, and not your aptitude, that determines your altitude."
Zig Ziglar

115. It's Not You, It's Me

Don't take things personally! This was the most meaningful career-related advice I ever received. New students will test you, and test you, and test you…You must develop thick skin, for if they sense blood, you are doomed. If there was a golden rule in teaching, not taking things personally would have to be it. (I use the term "golden rule" as opposed to the "rule of thumb" because I was once told the origin of the rule of thumb is that a while back, in England, a man used to be allowed to hit his wife as long as the instrument was no wider than his thumb.)

Now we come to one of the most fascinating phenomena known to teachers. Quick question: Which students are most likely to come back and visit you years later? Unbelievable, isn't it? The students who gave you the most difficulty are the ones you made the biggest impact on. The message is clear: Stay the course with those who need it most.

116. Pay Attention to Whom You Pay Attention.

80% of our interactions are with 20% of our students. In addition, chances are that your favorite students are your colleagues' favorites. In your own way, I challenge you to break this cycle that ignores the quiet mid-kids.

117. Bite Your Tongue!

Teachers talk too much. Who does most of the talking in your class? It is a simple question, but it says volumes about your teaching style. Better yet, who do your students learn the most from, you or their peers? On most levels, teachers talk way too much. Yes, these teachers are very bright and have important degrees to prove it, but most students don't care about that. Students will do better in a child-centered classroom where their thoughts and ideas guide the lesson. Students are influenced more by their peers, but an experienced teacher should be able to manipulate the progression of class in a way that the students' conversation covers the objectives of the lesson.

118. Phone Home?

Maintaining regular contact with home can be simple and effortless. How would you like to increase your communication with families by 100% without picking up a telephone? (There are ways to contact home without using your entire preparation period on the phone and in the process disturbing someone at work.) This task is simple due to the notion that most teachers communicate with less than ten percent of their students' families on a regular basis. Therefore, doubling this number (increasing it by 100%) can easily be achieved by sending a note home, when returned signed, is worth five bonus points.

Two days before every test, I hand out study guides containing the key terms and pertinent questions the students will need to study. The guide is set up in a way making it convenient for families to quickly quiz their children on the material and see how well they know the information. Before the students leave, we go over the guide and I ask if they have any questions. If they have it signed by an adult from their family on the day of the test, I award them with five points before they start the test. (I have had many parents tell me that they love this idea and they wished that more teachers would use the same method.)

Why does this work? People are always going to want something for nothing. Or as close to nothing as possible if it means they get a little extra than someone else.

119. X Marks the Spot

Most teachers have no immediate concrete consequences for student misbehavior. Aside from shouting and detention, which many students quickly become desensitized to, teachers set themselves up for most of their discipline problems. It may be hard to accept, but most of the problems teachers have, are ones they create for themselves.

Did your students ever take minutes to get ready for class? Did they ever start packing up their things while you were trying to bring closure to a lesson? And I repeat, most of the problems teachers have, are ones they create for themselves.

For the following actions, or inactions, my students receive an X. An X is one point off their final marking period averages. It sounds very simple, but it produces amazing results. In my grade book, I mark an X and place the date of the incident with a corresponding number reminding me which policy they broke.

Typical penalized infractions: Not starting their work within the first minute of class; something must be written. / Not doing any classwork. / Not bringing their textbooks when told. (I keep a daily sign outside my class.) / Sleeping (If their head is down or I can't see their eyes, it is sleeping.) Second offense results in a phone call home. / Writing on or destroying school property. / Packing up too early. / Reading material unrelated to school. / Reading or writing a note. / Playing with a toy, rubberband, jewelry, etc.../ Using cosmetics.

120. Don't Stand So Close to Me

Don't allow students to interrupt/sidetrack your lessons with trivial things. When I was a student, I clearly remember the peer praise a student would receive when she distracted the teacher from his dull lecture. It eventually turned into a game. Who could come up with a question related to the topic of discussion, which would take us the most off track?

Every day, every teacher, every class has interruptions. Most of these are minor infractions and many are simply attention-seeking behaviors. You need to extinguish them without skipping a beat from your lesson. To do this you need to become an expert in the psychology of physical proximity.

Most students will stop their misbehavior when they notice the teacher getting closer to them than normal. For me, physical proximity means that I make extended eye contact or use an unobtrusive tap on her desk. If these things don't work and the class is affected by the misbehavior, I take out my grade book and mark X's for the student until she focuses. I don't like assigning detention because it is not an immediate consequence. If the student doesn't seem to respond to any of these warnings, then I deviate from my lesson and happen to remember I forgot to tell them about the five-paragraph essay that I was going to assign this weekend, all while staring at the student involved. Quick students will catch on to what I am doing and tell the person to stop. It is a wonderful experience to see the expression on a student's face, who is seeking attention from her classmates, when the entire class turns on her in a matter of seconds.

121. Are You Active Enough?

Most problems a teacher has in the class are created by being reactive instead of proactive. How often do you stop problems before they happen? An experienced teacher will notice patterns that help him see problems before they manifest. The most important quality to possess as a teacher is to be proactive instead of reactive. Simply put, a proactive teacher knows what a student is thinking before she does. A term that connects well with the proactive teacher is "withitness." If you find yourself reacting to a problem, it is already too late.

122. Sorry Charlie!

Don't accept a simple "I'm sorry." If you are asking a student to apologize, hold her accountable for saying more than just "I'm sorry." An "I'm sorry" is a worthless, thoughtless response that doesn't challenge the student to consider what she did wrong.

123. Are You Threatening Me?

Make promises, not threats. You know the scene, "Jasmine, stop that or else. I'm serious Jasmine, if you don't stop it you will be in trouble." No matter the age, teachers really need to be concrete with their warnings. "Jasmine, if you don't stop playing with your necklace, you will be marked down for two X's." It sounds silly, but this way works better.

124. Name That Tune

When you say something once, don't expect it to sink in all the way. Question: What is your favorite song? Now think, what might your favorite song tell you about education? (Really contemplate this for a moment.)

Would you be able to sing along if you heard the song right now? Probably word for word. With that, have you heard the song more than once? One of the biggest mistakes teachers make is to teach something once and expect students to remember/comprehend it. Despite the idea that memorization has become the ultimate taboo in education today, you can't ignore the fact that repetition is a crucial part of learning.

I had a colleague tell me that he often uses the rule of two: For any key concept, review it two hours later, two days later, two weeks later, and two months later. (Obviously, this is not possible for most of us. I merely offer it as a model.)

125. Let's Be Friends

There is a huge difference between being friends and being friendly. As teachers, we need to draw this line and make it clear to our students that we are not their friends. (That may have come out meaner than I planned.) What I am trying to say is students need to develop healthy relationships with adults/authority figures and by being a student's friend it may eventually do more harm than good.

126. "Sit Down You're Rocking the Boat"

They really don't care what you think. Grin and bear it! Let me guess, you are a teacher with a few complaints and you could fix the major problems of your school within a month's time if you were in charge. The problem is very few people actually care. Yes, you and I are cogs in the machine. (Working for the man!) And the people who run this machine don't want to hear from you unless you have done something extraordinary.

I used to wonder about teacher burnout. I always had the feeling it wasn't the students who brought teachers to their breaking point. Face it, all schools are victims of politics, and chances are you aren't treated as the valuable asset you truly are to the school. Regardless of the facts, the people sitting in the air-conditioned rooms don't want to be bothered. Unless your problem is uncontrollable, or should involve an outside specialist, fix it yourself and stop complaining.

127. The Popular Vote

Don't try to be their favorite teacher. Early in my career I noticed it really bothered me if a student didn't like me. In fact, it became very important to me that every one of my students liked me, and liked me best. This created a huge mess for me. It is very normal to want to be liked and appreciated by your students, but you will get more from them if you resist this impulse. Be a fair, firm, and fun teacher and in the long run the students will like/respect you more for these qualities than any other.

128. O Captain, My Captain!

When team activities arise, refrain from picking captains. Do I need to explain why? Choose teams randomly or just read off the names. If they have a problem with the teams you picked, tell them to open their textbooks and begin reading chapter 12. They won't complain about it again.

129. Just Do as I Say, Don't Do as I Do

Don't eat or gossip in front of your students. And please don't be the teacher who drinks soda in front of them while they are working. At most, keep a water bottle on your desk because you never want to leave your classroom unattended.

This notion may sound too conservative, but when in doubt, follow the same rules as the students when it comes to food, cell phones, gum, etc...

130. Brain Teaser

The day before yesterday, Anton was 27 years old. Next year he will be 30 years old. How?

131. Multicultural Activity (Focusing on Trust)

Predator vs. Prey

Group size:	10-25
Age Group:	7 and up
Materials:	Blindfold and a plastic bottle/can with rocks in it
Time:	15 to 20 minutes
Location:	Gymnasium or outdoors
Skills:	Multicultural Appreciation, Cooperation, & Trust

a. The first thing you need to do is form a circle. Have students join hands to form a large circle. (Many students won't form a circle if you say "hold" hands.)

b. Explain to the students they are going to have the opportunity to partake in a trust activity. Tell them that trust activities mean they have to be very responsible so no one gets injured.

c. Inform the students that by forming a circle they have created a forest. In the forest there are predators and prey. (Ask for volunteers to describe the difference. You might also want to see what they know about the food chain.) In this activity the big predator will have to catch the small prey. The major challenge is that the predator must wear a blindfold because the small prey has an advantage in the chase.

d. Tell the students that even if they are not the predator or prey, they need to act as stationary trees warning the predator when she has moved too far near the periphery of the forest. Trees warn the predator by saying, not shouting, "tree."

e. Choose two volunteers. Blindfold the predator and hand the prey the shaker. When the predator is blindfolded, instruct the prey to shake when ready. Give the predator about one minute to devour the prey.

f. Process the activity: Which role was harder? What was so difficult about it?

132. Fascinating Fact

Sometimes lightning travels from the ground up.

133. An Important Thing I Learned About Life is...

The best time/place to floss your teeth is the shower.

Answer to #130—His birthday is December 31, the day is Jan. 1. The day before yesterday, Dec. 30, he was 27. On Dec. 31, yesterday, he turned 28. At the end of this year he will turn 29. Next year he will be thirty.

Chapter Eleven—Educational Theory

134. "I hear and I forget. I see and I remember. I do and I understand."
Confucius

135. **Have a Splendid Day!**

What is the telltale sign that you had a great school day? This year mine was during a lesson on the U.S. Civil War. Why? Not one of my ninety students asked for a hallway/bathroom pass during the entire day. I acquired a bunch of relics from a museum in South Carolina and the students were mesmerized.

Another indicator: How often do they leave class talking about the lesson?

136. **Make No Mistake**

It is okay to make mistakes! To go about teaching with the fear of messing up will eventually consume you. It never fails, when talking with new teachers, the biggest fear they express is what to do if they don't know the answer to a student's question about the curriculum.

On a related note, try using the phrase "guess and test" as opposed to "trial and error." The words we choose have a major influence on the atmosphere of the classroom.

On another related note, I once read that traditional Persian rugs have a deliberate, minor mistake woven into them. The belief being that nobody is perfect or should strive for perfection. (That being said, you may notice a few minor mistakes while reading this book.)

137. **To Make Learning Delicious**

While some people spend hours writing pages and pages about their philosophy of education, I believe it comes down to one idea: Teachers have the capability of making learning delicious.

138. **Through Thick and Thin**

Avoid asking students too many yes or no questions. They are at the bottom of the list when it comes to learning. They are also at the bottom of Bloom's

Taxonomy. I have always felt that one of the most challenging parts of being a teacher is finding the best questions to ask your students. Many teachers use the terms "thick" and "thin" questions to differentiate between higher-level thinking and lower-level thinking questions.

139. My Way or the Highway

Too much of what we teach goes down a one way street. I guess that is one of the major themes of this book. We have the answers, we give students the answers, and we expect them to remember/understand the answers. But when do they get to use these ideas in a creative or challenging way? (I hope you are not thinking of the chapter test.)

The question is simple: Do you create opportunities for your students to use what they learned in a worthwhile way? For every major theme/unit you teach, you have at your fingertips, and not metaphorically speaking, a way to take their learning to the next level. Remember, we are in the memory-making business.

For those who are ready to take a big step in this area, think Learn & Serve America. The latest Service Learning project I work on was titled "Fair Trade v. Free Trade." The students researched the issue, created a PowerPoint presentation for the entire school, and sold fair trade coffee for teachers in the morning, while handing out brochures they created. It was the most multifaceted project I was ever involved in, and the students did 95% of the work.

140. Are you a Pig?

What would be the first change you would make if your classes were all switched to accelerated classes? Same age, same curriculum. How about if you were given all students on the basic skills level? How would your attitude be different?

There was some research done where they randomly put together a few classes and told two of the teachers they were getting honors classes and the other two were told they were getting the low achievers. What do you think happened? The honors teachers' attitudes were better, there was less discipline problems, and the students performed significantly better. The teachers of the low performing students did much worse in all three categories. So what's the message? Too often we quickly label our students and this judgment lowers our expectations. Remember, as challenging as some of your students are supposed to be, they never had a teacher like you before. And sometimes all it takes is one.

This scenario is referred to as the Pygmalion effect or the self-fulfilling prophecy. "Pygmalion" refers to the George Bernard Shaw play in which the main character undergoes an amazing transformation based solely on another's high expectations.

141. When is the Best Time to Review?

Often. The better question is *where* is the best place to review? Math becomes so much more interesting when it is brought up in Language Arts class. Find out what information colleagues are going over in their classes, and when time allows, ask the students to explain some concepts to you. For some students, this will be the first time they become really interested in the material. This idea is important during state-testing time. If a student in your homeroom is taking the math part of the test in your room, and you're a Language Arts teacher, there is a decent chance this student has never thought about math in your room before. Maybe I am overreacting, but it couldn't hurt to do a few math problems here and there in your spare time.

142. Gimme a Break

Should we give students a break when it comes to grades? Definitely not during the first and third marking periods. If a student should fail the first marking period and you give her a break, she will give less effort during the next marking period and expect another break later. We are facing what many experts consider a "rising tide of mediocrity" in our school systems. We cannot afford to give out social promotions. If you believe that you are doing her a favor by boosting her average because she has a pleasant personality, please reconsider.

---

143. Brain Teaser

A man and his son are driving on a rainy night. As they are driving, another car runs a stop sign and they swerve out of the way. The man and his son hit a different car and are flung off the road. When the ambulance gets there they notice that the father wasn't wearing a seatbelt and he is dead. The son was wearing his seatbelt and was hurt badly. Soon after, the ambulance rushes the son to the hospital. When the son gets to the emergency room, the operation is about to start and the doctor stops and says, "I can't operate on this boy because he is my son." How is this possible?

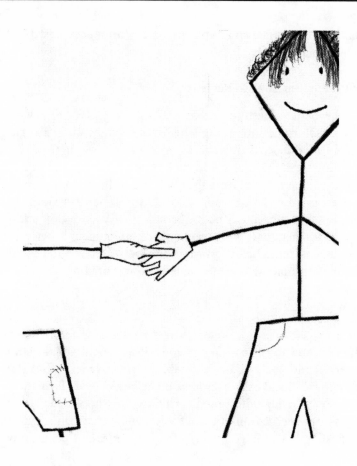

144. Multicultural Activity (Focusing on Multitasking)

Pull My Finger

Group size:	10-25
Age Group:	10 and up
Materials:	None
Time:	15 to 20 minutes
Location:	Classroom or outdoors
Skills:	Multicultural Appreciation, Perspective, & Fun

a. Have the students form a circle. Tell them to hold out their left hands, palms up and open. Tell them to hold their right hand out, sticking their pointer fingers out.

b. Tell them to stick their pointer finger on the palm of the person to their right. (Make sure all palms are flat.) Inform the students there is a defensive and offensive part for this activity. They need to make sure their finger doesn't get caught by the person on the right, and they need to try and catch the finger of the person on the left. When everyone has a flat palm, and a pointer finger touching it, the teacher calls out, "1, 2, 3, Lift!"

c. A finger must be caught for at least two seconds for the person to be out. I usually do a practice round so students get the idea and don't walk away upset because they didn't understand the rules.

d. Process this activity: What was the most difficult part of the activity? What does this activity have to do with school/life?

145. Fascinating Fact

An estimated 95% of the media you read, hear, and watch is owned/controlled by one of six mother companies. (AOL/Time Warner, Bertlesmann, Disney, News Corporation, Viacom, and Vivendi.)

146. An Important Thing I Learned About Life is…

Some people know the price of everything, but the value of nothing.

Answer to #143—The doctor is his mother.

Chapter Twelve—Time Management

147. "You can learn many things from children. How much patience you have, for instance." Franklin P. Jones

148. Feeling Down?

Principals love to see students hanging in your doorway a minute before the bell rings. In actuality, down time is *the* most detrimental moment in teaching. It leads to a lack of respect for your authority, and it opens the window for all sorts of discipline problems.

Yes, some lessons end earlier than anticipated. But this should never result in the students earning free time. Imagine what your principal would think if she stopped in and asked what was going on, and your only reply was you finished early and gave your students free time.

To avoid down time, don't wait till the last minute. Always have a backup activity. Give them spelling words, state capitals, etc... Eliminating down time is by no means an easy task. When I end a lesson early and don't know what to do, I grab a few D'Amato Dollars and in the seconds it takes to quiet the class down, I look around the room and find something to ask a few questions about.

149. Let's Go to the Videotape

There are two types of videos: Ones that work and those that don't. I am sure we have all been there. We have what we think is a phenomenal tape, we are excited to show it, and it FLOPS!

Experience is the only way around this problem. I suggest keeping a video library of tapes that "work." Each time you find one that really works, make a spare copy and stash it in your library. I suggest writing notes like how many minutes long the tape is before shelving it. I also write down what I felt were key questions to ask.

If the video has a questionable rating, send home permission slips. You don't need families calling up and bothering your principal.

The best video I have ever shown was "The Story of Ernest Green." So far, it was the only video my students clapped for at the end. (It is a Civil Rights Movement video from Disney, based on the Little Rock Nine. It is very moving and very accurate. I have used it successfully with both middle and high school students.) Bill Nye the Science Guy is also a hit with almost all ages.

150. Procrastinator

Did you type something at home that you need to hand out to your first period class? Let me guess, your photocopier tends to be broken down more than it is working properly. Don't stress and rush to work to get to the copy machine ten minutes before the other procrastinators. E-mail the document to yourself as an attachment, and if you can't get to the copier, just print out the document several times from the Internet and make additional copies during your preparation period. What if the Internet is down too, you ask? Then you really shouldn't have left this work till the last minute in the first place!

151. Been There, Done That

Most teachers experience major problems during the year, many of us on a daily basis. I am sure within the last week there have been a few times when you asked yourself, "Why me?" An important thing to remember is no matter how big, and how frequent your problems arise, there is someone who went through the same issues and survived. I guess what I am trying to say is don't take it upon yourself to reinvent the wheel. The solution to your problem is out there. When you talk with other colleagues about what you are going through, they tend to have a way to make your problems seem smaller. (Remember what stressed backwards spells.)

I once heard this tale that if you were sitting at a table with a dozen strangers and everyone was allowed to "dump" all of their problems on a plate, and then you were given the first pick of all the plates around you, you would take your plate back right away. True, you have problems, but they are your problems, and you're probably much closer to where you want to be than you think.

152. Sick Day v. Dear Day

Drop Everything And Read if you are feeling "out of it" and can't afford to miss a day of work. Special note: A poorly organized Dear Day will wind up being worse than a regular day of classes. To ensure a quality and stress-free Dear Day you need to establish a few rules: You may only switch books once, no sharing books, no writing during the period, no magazines/yearbooks, and no talking.

Dear Days go much smoother if you have saved books over time and created a "classroom library." Save your weekly readers, subscribe to an age appropriate, curriculum-related magazine. (Kids Discover are fantastic for Language Arts, Science, and Social Studies.)

In the morning of a Dear Day, when I see students in the hallway, I will let them know to bring something to read for later. This way they don't ask to go to their locker at the beginning of class. I also like to put a sign out sheet for when students borrow my books. I believe it helps to deter the vandalism of my books.

153. Reach Out and Touch Someone

The quantity and quality of professional interaction in schools is unsatisfactory. Schools do not make enough effort to allow teachers to network, plan together, or even discuss common issues.

A list serve is an Internet tool that offers teachers a new arena to share ideas with each other via e-mail. At my school, over twenty-five teachers write to each other about upcoming events, issues in the school, and current things in the news. The way a list serve works is you find a host site (we use topica.com) and one person opens a free account. Then the person enters the e-mail addresses of those who want to be part of the list serve. Once everyone accepts the e-mail from the host site, anyone can send an e-mail to the address, and everyone who signed up gets a copy. It offers teachers communication with colleagues they might have gone the whole year without talking to.

154. Work Smarter, Not Harder

Often in life we overcomplicate our problems. Yes, we all have daily challenges. But that does not mean the solution is spending hours to fix it. The most successful teachers are the ones who are the most resourceful. Instead of staying after school for several hours trying to improve your situation, talk to your colleagues, check out ideas on the Internet, or pick up a book on teaching.

---

155. Brain Teaser

Where has every king of England been crowned?

156. Multicultural Activity (Focusing on Cliques)

Cliques
Group size:	7-20
Age Group:	8 and up
Materials:	None
Time:	15 to 20 minutes
Location:	Outdoors or gymnasium
Skills:	Multicultural Appreciation, Conflict Resolution, & Team Building

a. Have the students join hands to make a circle. Have a volunteer leave the circle. Tell the volunteer she has to break through the circle and get into the middle. Her main rules are she cannot jump over the circle or lead with her head, elbows, or shoulders.

b. The rest of the group has to do its best to prevent the person from getting in the circle.

c. Process the activity: What does this activity have to do with school/life? What thoughts were going through your head as you attempted to get in the circle?

157. Fascinating Fact

In an average year, more people are killed by donkeys than are killed in plane crashes.

158. An Important Thing I Learned About Life is...

It is best to look at all people as fellow travelers.

Answer to #155—On the head.

Chapter Thirteen—Miscellaneous

159. "The nail that sticks out is hammered down." Japanese proverb

160. Are You Nuts?

Of course not! You were smart enough to choose this book, right? Actually you need to ask this question each time you bring treats for your students. I have been at work before when an ambulance had to be called due to a student eating something with peanuts she wasn't supposed to. Apparently, many schools are banning nut products due to the growing number of students deathly allergic to nuts.

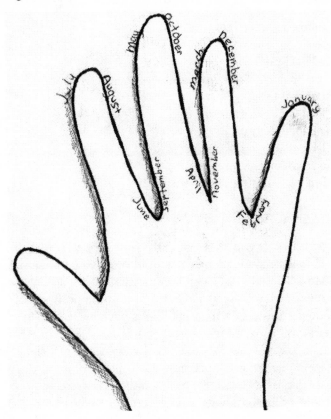

161. Let Your Fingers Do the Walking

To teach the months, have students hold out a hand. Point to your pinky, it is January, it has 31 days. Drag your finger down the valley between the pinky and the next finger, that is February, it doesn't have 31 days. Pull your finger up to the tip of the finger after the pinky, that is March, it has 31 days. Drag your finger to the valley…do this till you get to your pointer finger, it gets hit twice as July and August, both have 31 days. Now go backwards, placing you in the valley between the pointer and middle finger, September does not have 31 days…

For multiplying a single digit by nine, hold up both of your hands, fingers spread out. Pick a number one through nine. Let us say you picked three. From the left, count to your third finger, put it down. The answer to nine times three should be a two digit number. The first digit is how many fingers are standing to the left of the finger that is down. The second digit is the number of fingers standing to the right of the finger that is down.

162. Misnomers

Answer the following questions:

Who is buried in Grant's tomb?
What word comes next, "Four score and seven years ago, our…?"
Who sewed the first U.S. flag?
What came first, the chicken or the egg?
What is the smallest country in the world?
What is the largest lake in the world?
Who was the youngest U.S. president?
What is the longest-running Broadway play?

163. Are You a Show Off?

Your principal wants you to be one. Take your very best work, like the outstanding posters your students made, and decorate your classroom and hallways with them. (I usually get them laminated at school so they last longer.) My principal prefers they are graded and have some positive comments on them. My students' posters on the Civil Rights Movement "Top Seven Project" came out so nice they wound up decorating our school's main office. The students were ecstatic when they saw their work outside the principal's room.

On another note, my principal stopped in my room one day to ask me something and became distracted when he noticed my screen savers were digital photographs of my students actively involved with a task. After about twenty seconds he looked at me, sort of like he forgot what he came for, smiled, and left.

164. A Novel Idea

For an entire marking period I had a handful of students reading a novel a week, and begging for more. Oh, I forgot to mention, they were seventh graders.

There is a series of books called Classics Illustrated. CI puts out illustrated novels, like <u>Don Quixote</u>, <u>Hamlet</u>, and <u>Uncle Tom's Cabin</u>, that can be read in less than an hour. The books are not original texts, but what a head start you can give a student with these books. Their cover price is $4.95, but I have bought them at 99-cent stores and Internet auction sites for a dollar each. (I believe there are over fifty books in the new series from the 1990's.) I leave these books on the chalkboard ledge and the students flock to them.

165. Every Good Boy Deserves…

Mnemonics!!! Mnemonic devices are short cuts in learning. They offer a slick way of remembering important facts and concepts. Let's see how you do with these:

a. My Very Educated Mother Just Served Us Nasty Pizza
b. HOMES
c. Roy G. Biv
d. King Philip Climbed Over Five Great Stones
e. FANBOYS
f. CAN'T
g. Please Excuse My Dear Aunt Sally
h. Right Tight, Left Loose
i. Whites Warm, Colors Cold

166. Ready for a Promotion?

Look to promote your school. Put out a press release about an upcoming project to a newspaper or television network, get your students to enter an essay-writing contest, or find a nearby business willing to create a scholarship for your school. Your principal will think highly of you when she includes it in her end of the year highlights that have to be submitted to the superintendent.

167. Fear Factor

Give your students a chance to pick up a dead animal. Get a big box (one of those boxes that holds copy paper will do) and cut a hole in the top. Write "Caution: Dead Animal" in big letters on the side. Tell your students that the animal is definitely dead and they won't get hurt or sick by touching it. Randomly pick students to put a blindfold on and stick their hands in the box. (I don't ask for volunteers for this activity because the bravest go first and it quickly reduces the excitement when they touch the animal nonchalantly.) By the way, the animal is a coral. Activities like this make for wonderful writing assignments. Let them write about their feelings before and after they touch it. (Remember, we are in the memory-making business.)

It is a good idea to keep up with pop-culture. It builds on your student rapport and gives you a reasonable excuse to watch shows like the MTV Music Awards.

---

168. Brain Teaser

What is the pattern? 8,5,4,9,1,7,6,3,2,0

169. Multicultural Activity (Focusing on Expression of One's Creativity)

Honey, Do You Love Me?

Group size:	8-25
Age Group:	7 and up
Materials:	None
Time:	15 to 20 minutes
Location:	Classroom or outdoors
Skills:	Multicultural Appreciation, Public Speaking, & Fun

a. This activity is a competition where the winner is the last one standing.

b. Pick volunteers, one at a time, to ask other members sitting in the circle, "Honey, do you love me?" The asking students should be encourage to "ham it up."

c. If the person asked can reply, maintaining eye contact, and without laughing or smiling, within ten seconds, "Honey, I love you, but you are not going to make me smile," then that person is still in the game.

d. Process the activity: Which role was more difficult? What strategy did you use to make sure you were successful?

170. Fascinating Fact

Alabama's constitution still calls for separate schools for "white and colored children." In the November 2004 elections, an amendment to change this idea was defeated.

171. An Important Thing I Learned About Life is...

Don't flush public toilets with your hands.

Answers to #162—Tombs are above ground, hence no one is <u>buried</u> there. / It is just "fathers," not forefathers. / The first flag was not sewn by Betsy Ross. / Dinosaurs laid eggs long before there were chickens. / Vatican City is the smallest country in the world. / The Caspian Sea is the largest lake in the world. / Theodore Roosevelt became president at 42, Kennedy became president at 43. / There isn't a longest-running play: People read plays and watch productions.

Answers to #165:

a. The planets in order from the sun (Mercury, Venus, Earth, Mars, Jupiter, Saturn, Uranus, Neptune, Pluto)

b. The Great Lakes (Huron, Ontario, Michigan, Erie, Superior)

c. The colors of the rainbow (Red, Orange, Yellow, Green, Blue, Indigo, Violet)

d. Classification of Organisms (Kingdom, Phylum, Class, Order, Family, Genus, Species)

e. Coordinating conjunctions (For, And, Nor, But, Or, Yet, So) f. The four states that border Mexico (California, Arizona, New Mexico, Texas)

g. The order of mathematical operations (Parentheses, Exponents, Multiply, Divide, Add, Subtract)

h. Tightening or loosening a knob.

i. The type of water you should use when doing your laundry of colors and whites.

Answer to #168—Alphabetical order.

Chapter Fourteen—The End is Near

172. "Children require guidance and sympathy far more than instruction."
Annie Sullivan

173. What's Your Fantasy?

The Fantasy Island project is the perfect closure project for the end of the year. It allows the students a chance to show off what they learned in your class. This model can easily be changed to fit your class curriculum.

Overview—On a journey across the globe you happened to discover an island. Being the founder(s) of the island, you are entitled to claim this island. For this project you will present your island as it is ten years from when you first discovered it.

You should include several of the following:
a.   When and how it was found
b.   How it was settled
c.   Who immigrated there, how and why?
d.   Type of government
e.   Fads (Clothing, entertainment, music, television, etc...)
f.   Transportation
g.   Population
h.   Schools
I.   Longitude and Latitude
j.   Climate / Weather
k.   Imports and exports
l.   Natural Resources
m.   Current and historical events
n.   Other (Airports, animals, armed forces, court system, garbage, harbors, holidays, occupations, mail, markets, museums, police, sewage, technology, telephone, water, etc..)

You need to physically construct the following in a creative and unique way:
a.   Currency

b.   Flag
c.   Genealogy
d.   Constitution (With a preamble and at least five amendments)
e.   Map
f.   Pictures of your inhabitants
g.   Brochure (Include geographical features, tourist sites, landmarks, landmasses, and bodies of water.)

174. Pick Your Battles

You can't solve every problem or resolve every issue. Intelligent teachers develop a sixth sense for distinguishing between problems worth fighting for, and those they should just let slide.

175. Share the Wealth

The majority of the ideas in this book were accumulated from colleagues over the years. Every teacher I know has his own bag of tricks. I bet right now you could think of a couple things you love to do with your students that really impress them. These things are gold! These are the things that make you special to your students. Most importantly, these are the things that make the difference between having a student look forward to, or dread going to school.

176. Ciao, Grazie!

It is extremely important teachers offer their students some sort of closure during the last days of school. Many of our students have loved ones leaving their lives regularly and that often leads to emotional baggage. My suggestion is to try one of the simple activities listed in this book as a good-bye activity. I always end with a closure activity for the reasons stated above and also for the student who moves over the summer and I never get to see again. Teachers also need closure activities to say good-bye to those they grew close to over the year.

Before our time together comes to a close, I would like to express my warm gratitude. Thank you for giving my ideas a chance and I hope you enjoyed our journey together.

---

177. Brain Teaser

How come Eskimos never hunt penguins?

178. Multicultural Activity (Focusing on Conflict Resolution)

<u>Corporate Ladder</u>

Group size:	10-25
Age Group:	8 and up
Materials:	25 pieces of paper / A piece of paper with the solutions on it
Time:	20 to 25 minutes
Location:	Large classroom or outdoors
Skills:	Multicultural Appreciation, Communication, & Conflict Resolution

a. Have the students sit around the playing field, twenty-five pieces of paper spread out in a five by five shape. Leave about a foot between each paper.

b. The objective of the game is to figure out a preset pattern that will get a student from a starting "X" to the ending "X." (The starting "X" and the ending "X" are the corners opposite of each other.)

c. The main rule of the game is that you can move up, down, left, or right. The student will not have to touch a square that has already been stepped on. The only way a student gets a strike is if she doesn't leave the maze the same way she went through it after making a mistake. If the students can reach the end before getting three strikes, the students win. Three strikes and the teacher wins.

d. As the student takes each step, you will look at your chart and tell her whether or not she made a right move. She keeps going until she makes a wrong step, then the next person goes. Have about four patterns ready for a twenty minute period. The patterns should start off somewhat easy and increase in difficulty as the students get better. Process the activity.

179. Fascinating Fact

Franklin Delano Roosevelt was chosen to be on the dime due to his association with the March of Dimes. (The March of Dimes was the organization that fought against polio, the disease that crippled him.)

180. An Important Thing I Learned About Life is…

As teachers, first we help our students find their roots, then we help them strengthen their wings.

Answer to #177—Eskimos, or the "Nunavut," live near the North Pole. Penguins do not naturally live above the Equator.

0-595-33783-X

Printed in the United States
83631LV00005B/4-15/A